Beautifully Digging Deeper

Tonia Dockery-Mierez
Guest Author: Hailee Mooney

Published by: Tonia Dockery-Mierez

Copyright © 2025 Tonia Dockery-Mierez

All rights reserved

All rights reserved. No part of this publication may be reproduced, distributed, or transmitted in any form. This includes photocopying, recording, or other electronic or mechanical methods. Prior written permission from the publisher is required. Brief quotations in critical reviews are an exception.
For permissions, write to the publisher, addressed "Attention: Permissions Coordinator" at the address below.
Ordering Information: Quantity sales. Discounts are available on quantity purchases by corporations, associations, and others. For details, contact the publisher at the address above. Orders by U.S. trade bookstores and wholesalers. Please contact:
beautifullydiggingdeeper@gmail.com
Printed in the United States of America Publisher's Cataloging-in-Publication data Tonia Dockery-Mierez.

Beautifully Digging Deeper / Tonia Dockery-Mierez with Hailee Mooney.

ISBN: 979-8-9986615-0-1

1. Christianity & Spirituality — Women's Inspirational.
2. Christian Living — From Self-Help Topics.
3. Health and Wellness, and Women's Studies.

[Library of Congress Classification Number (pending)]
[Library of Congress Control Number (pending)]
First Edition

What is Inside?

Preface

Chapter 1 | Who Am I Anyway?
    Digging Deeper...
    Dry Bones?
    Who is she?
    The Journey Continues...
    Actions and Behavior:
    This Week's Confession:

Chapter 2 | God Loves Smoothies
    Busting Out of My Jeans!
    My Miracle Machine
    Gaining Momentum
    Made in His Image

Chapter 3 | He Will Lead
    My Plans are not always God's Plans
    Is Spiritual Depression Real?
    <u>His Plan Was Crystal Clear</u>
    <u>Embrace Authenticity</u>
    <u>Deliver Twelve Lessons</u>
    <u>Goals for the Week</u>
    <u>This Week's Confession</u>

Chapter 4 | Prayer Only Refuse Worry
    Spiritual Depression | Let Us Talk About It...
    Coping with Spiritual Depression
    Healing and Hope
    How To Actually Do It
    Goals For the Week
    This Weeks Confession

Chapter 5 | Validation Vortex
    Hard Cold Facts...
    Understanding Your Worth
    Life Stories FROM incredible women...
    Moving Beyond the Struggle:
    Consequences of Not Moving Beyond:

    Goals for the Week
    This Week's Confession
    About our Co-author

Chapter 6 | Slavery to Freedom
    Is Praise and Worship a Key?
    Taking Responsibility for My Own Actions?
    Conscientious Choices

Chapter 7 | Beauty takes time
    The Power of Routines
    The Hard Work Behind the Glow
    Consistency is Key
    Time: The Most Valuable Investment

Chapter 8 | Defining Diva Your Way
    1. Driven
    2. Inspiring
    3. Victorious
    4. Actionable
    Preparation with Purpose
    Daily Reflection
    [A Queenly Influence](#)

Chapter 9 | Walking In Your Esther Moment
    Accept your calling!
    Resolve to take the leap of faith—no matter the outcome!
    Let God deal with your enemies!

Chapter 10 | A Personal Call to Action
    Unleashed Purpose
    Deeper Relationships
    Legacy of Hope
    The Joy of the Lord is Your Strength!
    [Acknowledgements](#)

Preface

Beauty is not defined by what you see in the mirror. No matter how often people discuss you or your outward attractiveness, or how many jaws drop and breaths taken away. These are not the accurate measures of your beauty, as your true essence and magnificence go far beyond what words can describe.

Every morning, we look into the mirror, often seeking validation in our reflection, hoping to glimpse beauty as defined by the world. For years, I followed the same patterns and routines without questioning them. I spent countless hours focusing on the outward, convinced that true worth was something that others could see and measure. But then, everything changed in ways I could never have imagined.

It was the first time I saw myself from God's perspective. I perceived immense value, love, and purpose, not just physical form. In that moment, I realized God's perception of beauty in each of us transcends outward appearances and originates deep within our hearts, spirits, and actions. This revelation became the starting point of the Beautiful Movement in my heart. Significant milestones began to unfold, following that transformative experience.

This book is a testament to the incredible journey that I have embarked together with people of like mind.

This Beautiful Journey will explore the vital link between nourishing our bodies and spiritual well-being. We will journey together to discover wholesome food. Beyond this, we will embrace and celebrate the beauty that lies within each other. Through our shared stories, struggles, and triumphs, we will find strength in our faith and in the supportive community we have built.

One important thing that should radiate throughout the words, begin to look for the beauty in those around you. Speak life to them and trust in their goodness.

We have witnessed the blossoming of beauty, both in ways that are immediately visible and in subtle transformations that some may not yet realize. Others have felt and seen these changes, both inside and out.

With guidance from scripture and practical wisdom, we will discover what makes each of us uniquely beautiful. We will learn that our worth comes from our Creator's unconditional love, not society's standards. This book shares these lessons and experiences, offering a guide for others on their journey to self-discovery and empowerment.

As you read these pages, I invite you to see yourself as God sees you: beautiful, valuable, and capable of incredible things. Find inspiration in these stories and insights. Shake yourself and awaken to your inner beauty, nourish your body and soul, and live confidently, knowing you are beautiful. This is not just my journey—it is ours, a shared path filled with mutual growth and discovery. Together, we can redefine beauty and embrace the divine worth that lies within each of us.

If I could encourage you to do one thing, slow down and consume the read.

Chapter 1 | Who Am I Anyway?

If we could only get it right the first time. If only we were the perfect version of character, mind, body and soul straight out of the gate.

Write your vision, make it plain.

We spend so much time focused on everyone else; don't you think it is time to give yourself a little focus?

No, I am not talking about your daily skincare rituals or the makeup routine, or the time you take every day getting your hair exactly right. Sister, we have that down to science. Afterall, we are all beauty consultants, aren't we?

Have you ever gazed into yourself beyond just the mirror? How long has it been since you have looked beyond the mirror?

Have you ever examined what makes you, you?

Underneath the flowing hair, getting deeper than the Lucious lips, cruise beyond those swaying hips momma and just stop it with the catwalk strut. If you were to lose all those things tomorrow, what would define you? Do you have anything to give of yourself beyond beauty?

It is the Intelligence...

Ah, Intelligence, you say! So, you are smarter than most? What good would that intelligence do if this were your last week on earth?

CHAPTER 1 | WHO AM I ANYWAY?

There is so much more within you, there is a deeper realm within yourself.

Beyond your surface-self lives your true self, yearning for expression. How long have you been feeling outwardly beautiful but inwardly bland, stale, pale, or simply dull?

You might be the opposite: confident on the inside but insecure about your image.

Time for honest self-reflection?

DIGGING DEEPER...

Is there a more rewarding experience than having a heart-to-heart chat with a friend? Have you ever met someone that you could simply bare your soul to without shame? Have you ever done that with yourself? Dormant states and dark spaces exist within your soul, places you may never have visited.

What about those long, luscious legs? Irrelevant at this moment...

In tune with my soul!

Imagine living a life where you were so intimately in tune with your soul and your heart that you could discern what was coming around the corner of your life in floods. Yes, that is a big statement, yet it's profoundly true because when you bring light to the *hidden places* within yourself, change is inevitable. We stagnate and maintain the status quo when we keep the inward shades drawn and refuse to see the ugly. The constant struggle to "get past" a thing—could this be because of the blinds we have drawn on the dark places in our spirit?

Outward giggles that hide inward turmoil.

For YOU is it...

Loneliness, Anger, Fear, Frustration, Anxiety, Depression, Sickness, Hate, Bitterness, Intimidation, Self-doubt, Insecurity, Shame, Resentment?

These things cause years of anguish and, according to God (Yahweh), "*dry the bones.*" Do you know what happens when the bones go dry?

DRY BONES?

Often associated with Proverbs 17:22 "A cheerful heart is marvelous medicine, but a crushed spirit dries up the bones" NIV.

In this context, a broken, discouraged, or sorrowful spirit profoundly affects someone's physical and mental health and well-being. *Lack of joy or hope* creates a deep connection between emotional and spiritual well-being and physical health; this deficiency causes lifelessness and physical deterioration. Conversely, a cheerful heart brings vitality and health to the body. Confronting and healing our hidden selves opens the path to genuine well-being, illuminating our lives with divine light and joy.

For many years, we have been deceiving ourselves about who we really are. By transforming ourselves into what others expect, we play the role of the "good little girl" to fit in. Masking our inner emptiness and longing for something real, we walk around like puppets, exuding false facades of joy.

He tells you every day about how good you smell and that your eyes are beautiful. Why is it we struggle so deeply to understand that true beauty has nothing to do with the outside?

The Internal Conflict

This internal conflict can lead to both inward and outward ugliness. Until we can truly listen to God's voice and be honest with ourselves, the hardness that the enemy is nurturing in our hearts will continue, leading us to grow colder, more shadowed, and more isolated.

Jayme

Consider Jayme's story, a brave girl who faced unimaginable darkness yet found her way back to the light. In 2018, someone abducted Jayme after she witnessed her parents' murder. Her captor's 88-day captivity destroyed her sense of self, subjugating her to his will. Jayme, even with the terror and manipulation, found her inner strength. A hope that defied her circumstances guided her escape and her run towards freedom.

A powerful testament to the human spirit's resilience and the importance of self-discovery is Jayme's story. In the darkness, she held onto a spark of her true self and an inner voice that validated her strength, proving her to be more than a victim. Her courageous escape and plea for help shattered the chains of fear and deception, representing profound *self-honesty and bravery*.

Just as Jayme did, let us silence the world's distractions and heed God's quiet guidance within. Shedding the masks we wear is the only way we can embrace the beauty of who we truly are. Even in the darkest times, Jayme's story shows that a path back to the light exists through self-truth and divine guidance.

> *"You are altogether beautiful, my love; there is no flaw in you." - Song of Solomon 4:7. You reflect the divine craftsmanship of our Creator by nurturing your mind, body, and spirit. Embrace your true self.*

WHO IS SHE?

What about my Outside?

Close your eyes and picture how you look. Now, honestly answer these questions about who you think you are. It's time to rediscover and celebrate your unique beauty.

1. Who is she? By the way, she = You.

- Go beyond your own perspective and consider how others perceive you as well.
- Ensure your answers are genuine.

- How would you describe her in a few words?
- What is her temperament?

Notes

_____
_____
_____
_____

2. What do you want her to look like?

- How does she present herself to the world?
- What kind of energy does she radiate?

Notes

_____
_____
_____
_____

3. How does she interact with others?

- What kind of friend, partner, and family member is

she?

- How does she interact and form connections with those around her?

Notes

_____
_____
_____
_____

4. How does she express her creativity?

- In what ways does she engage in creative pursuits?

- Does she allow herself the freedom to explore and experiment?

Notes

_____
_____
_____
_____

5. What is her relationship with her body?

- How does she feel about her physical appearance and health?

- Is she mindful of her body's needs and signals?

Notes

_____
_____
_____
_____

Now let us walk through the inside of our Inward Qualities

1. Who is she?

- What are her core values and beliefs?

Notes

_____
_____
_____
_____

2. Is she gentle and kind?

- How does she show compassion and empathy?

- In what ways does she practice self-care and kindness towards herself?

Notes

_____
_____
_____
_____

3. Is she hard or soft?

   - Does she show strength and resilience?

   - Does she have a gentle, nurturing demeanor?

   - How does she balance assertiveness and gentleness?

Notes

_____
_____
_____
_____

4. Is she trustworthy?

   - How does she build and maintain trust with others?

   - Is she reliable, both to herself and to others?

Notes

5. Is she bitter?

   - Does she hold on to past grievances or resentments?

   - How does she work towards forgiveness and letting go of negativity?

   Notes

6. What are her dreams and aspirations?

   - What are her long-term goals and passions?

   Notes

7. How does she handle challenges and setbacks?

   - What is her approach to overcoming obstacles?

   - Does she learn from her mistakes and grow stronger?

   - Does she shrivel up and die?

   - Maybe she fights like a lion?

Notes

_____
_____
_____
_____

8. What is her relationship with herself like?

   - How does she view her self-worth and self-esteem?

      - Is she at ease when she's alone and thinking deeply?

      - Is she comfortable in social settings?

Notes

_____
_____
_____
_____

9. What brings her joy and fulfillment?

- What activities and experiences make her feel alive and happy?

- How does she incorporate these into her daily life?

- Does she do anything that brings her joy?

Notes

_____
_____
_____
_____

10. How does she manage stress and maintain balance?

- What techniques and practices do she use to stay centered and calm?

- How does she prioritize her well-being?

Notes

_____
_____
_____
_____

What do you want her to look like?

Proverbs 21

In a small town in Georgia, nestled between thriving cities with vibrant streets, lived a woman named Tonia (that is me). My journey was nothing short of extraordinary, marked by a radical transformation as I sought and followed God's Divine guidance. From the beginning of my life, I faced several challenges and lived in complete disdain because of the massive amount of weight that I struggled to lose. One day, I had a piercing revelation of God's Word.

People knew me for my powerful will and unshakable faith, but I often struggled with deep insecurities about my appearance. This insecurity affected both my daily life and my walk with Christ. Despite my many acts of kindness and love for others, I saw myself as ugly on the outside and invisible on the inside. My silent battle continued until a wise, fiery woman named Rita entered my life.

Rita, a beacon of faith and wisdom, noticed my inner turmoil and confronted it head-on. With a voice that could move mountains, she says, "Tonia, your beauty shines brighter than the flashing lights of any city. But you need to see yourself as God sees you."

Though humbled and skeptical, my response was, "Thank you, Rita, but I struggle to see that beauty in myself."

Rita, undaunted, shared the powerful words of Proverbs 21:2: "Every way of a man is right in his own eyes, but the Lord weighs the heart." She painted a vivid picture of how God saw me — her heart for God and unshakable grit were her true beauty, far beyond the superficial.

Rita's words inspired me to dive into prayer and God's word with renewed fervor, seeking divine perspective and guidance. Days turned into years, and a remarkable transformation took root. My radiance became undeniable. One of two things happened, people were either drawn to me like a magnet, or they avoided me like the plauge. Regardless the stand they took many people sought wisdom and counsel through the God inside me.

Do the Mirrors Lie?

Maybe years passed and one pivotal evening, driven by a divine nudge, I stood before a mirror, hands trembling. As I gazed at my reflection, tears streamed down my face. The woman staring back was not the hideous figure I once knew, but a vessel of God's overwhelming grace and beauty. The person I saw looking back at me was the woman I met on the inside a few years back. I saw my eyes with a sparkle like diamonds and with a fierce kindness. My smile was a beacon of warmth, and my lips were beautiful as they voiced the lyrics to the most powerful melody that came from deep within my soul. My entire being emanated the love that had reshaped my *mind.*

Overwhelmed with joy, I remembered the words of Proverbs 21:21: "Whoever pursues righteousness and love finds life, prosperity, and honor." God had not only transformed my outward appearance but had unveiled my true essence—beautiful and radiant in *His* eyes.

Following that, I walked confidently, living Proverbs 21:3: God values righteousness and justice above sacrifice. I choose for my life to be a testament to the unstoppable power of God's Word and His transformative calling. Here am I Lord, send me, now aware that my inner beauty reflects God's unending love.

THE JOURNEY CONTINUES...

Just like you, I am a work in progress. My journey continues to blaze like wildfire through the pathway that He leads, igniting hope and inspiring others to seek the beauty that only God can reveal. My story is not just a tale of weight loss; it was a revolution of the soul, a testament to the power of divine truth, and a beacon that encourages others to step into the light and embrace their God-given beauty.

External Self:

Consider the timeless wisdom of Proverbs 31:30: "Charm is deceitful, and beauty is fleeting; but a woman who fears the LORD is to be praised."

Reflect deeply on these questions:

- Inner Beauty vs. External Appearance: Do you prioritize cultivating inner beauty and character, which endure beyond fleeting physical traits?

- Presentation to Others: How do you choose to present yourself to the world? Does your character shine brighter than your outward appearance?

- Contentment with Physical Appearance: Do you find peace with your physical appearance, understanding that God's design and purpose for you reflects true beauty?

- Judgment of Others: Do you judge others based on their external features, or do you see them through the lens of God's love and grace? - Read that again.

These reflections invite us to value qualities that endure and show God's heart rather than fleeting attributes that fade with time.

Notes

_____
_____
_____
_____

ACTIONS AND BEHAVIOR:

Proverbs 21:3–To do what is right and just is more acceptable to the LORD than sacrifice.

- Consider how your actions align with God's standards of righteousness.

- What actions define you in the eyes of others?

- Are you kind, honest, and respectful?

- How do your actions impact those around you?

Notes

_____
_____
_____
_____

Material Success:

Proverbs 11:28–Those who trust in their riches will fall, but the righteous will thrive like a green leaf.

- Evaluate whether you seek contentment in material possessions or in your relationship with God.

- How much importance do you place on wealth, possessions, and success?

- Are you content with what you have, or do you constantly crave more?

Notes

_____
_____
_____
_____

Internal Self:

Heart and Motives:

Proverbs 4:23–Above all else, guard your heart, for everything you do flows from it.

- Examine your motives and intentions, seeking alignment with God's will.

- What motivates your decisions and actions?

- Are your intentions pure, or do you harbor hidden agendas?

- How do you align your heart with God's will?

Notes

Character and Integrity:

Proverbs 10:9 states, those who walk in integrity walk securely, but those who take crooked paths will be found out.

- Prioritize honesty, even when it is challenging.

- How do you measure your integrity?

- Do you consistently choose righteousness over convenience?

- Are you honest even when no one is watching?

Notes

Emotional Landscape:

Proverbs 14:30–A heart at peace gives life to the body, but envy rots the bones.

- Cultivate inner peace, forgiveness, and joy.

- How do you handle emotions like anger, jealousy, and pride?

- Are you quick to forgive or hold grudges?

- Do you seek inner peace and joy?

Notes

_____
_____
_____
_____

Remember, Proverbs 21 teaches us that God values righteousness over sacrifices. Reflecting on both our inner and outer selves can bring powerful transformation.

Notes

_____
_____
_____
_____

This Week's Confession:

All things work together for *my* good. I will transform *my* pain into laughter, exchange *my* cross for a crown, and transform *my* mourning into dancing. I am blessed, and I am a blessing. My past disappointments will become testimonies in the name of Jesus.

> *"Healing will come for those around you, but God appointed you! Should you remain silent at this critical juncture, the Jews will find deliverance elsewhere, while you and your kinsmen face death. Who knows if perhaps this time has appointed you Queen?" (Esther 4:14, NLT)*

> *"Do not let any part of your body become an instrument of evil to serve sin. Instead, give yourselves completely to God, for you were dead, but now you have a new life. So, use your whole body as an instrument to do what is right for the glory of God." (Romans 6:13, NLT)*

Finding out who we are in Him takes giving up certain desires or habits that keep us from His perfect will. Stepping into the unknown, *our* "unknown" is a scary but vital part of understanding what God has planned for our future. Most times, we think our unknowns are unattainable. We see ourselves through the eyes of *can't* and *unqualified*. Instead, we should understand that our uniqueness is the God-gifts within us, making us amply qualified for the true "us" He has made us to be.

Note: What changes can I apply to my life and how will I begin a transformation?

_____
_____
_____

Self honesty is the first step toward healing.

I mean, who would have ever thought that the Lord would order a smoothie? But I am a firm believer that God loves smoothies...

Chapter 2 | God Loves Smoothies

BUSTING OUT OF MY JEANS!

Muffin Tops Galore

Life. Why does it have to be this way?

Ever feel like your jeans are conspiring against you? I swear mine has a secret meeting every time I walk past the fridge. It is like they are plotting to make me an unwilling member of the muffin top club!

While the context of this chapter speaks heavily about nutrition, read the words with the understanding that beyond the fridge and the struggle to be thin, getting to know His plan for you is the ultimate prize.

Ever feel you are constantly at war with your wardrobe? No matter what you try, those jeans always seem to be a size too small, revealing your muffin tops to everyone. Personally, that is why I do not wear jeans when I'm feeling large. I just cannot do it. See, you are not alone. Life feels like relentless pressure conforming to an ideal.

> *"Life, the struggle to fit into the mold, kind of like trying to squeeze a watermelon into a grape-sized mold.*

As someone whose brain is always on the move, jumping from one idea to the next, planning the future while juggling the present, I get it. The constant hustle may make it seem impossible to prioritize self-care, let alone your health. But what if we could change that? What if we could harmonize our active minds with a healthy routine that feels enjoyable?

> *I'm the Olympic champion of overthinking.*

> *I juggle ideas faster than I juggle my grocery list!*

> *"Therefore, whether you eat or drink, or whatever you do, do all to the glory of God."–1 Corinthians 10:31*

What? Does God care about what we eat? He said to eat or drink to His glory. Wow, that is an eye-opening picture for sure.

"This verse always makes me wonder: Is there a heavenly scale where God weighs our smoothies against our ice cream? If that's true, I'll require a significant amount of 'grace' to offset it!"

As someone who is always busy, I also do *not* enjoy cooking. I would rather spend my *time* with my family... (some of you might throw things at me for this one...) cooking for my family seems like a waste of precious time. If I am cooking, it should be a family event. We should do it together. My daughter and grandson would be all about that. Meanwhile, my husband is like a kitchen ninja—swift and deadly with a spatula, and not keen on sharing the spotlight!

Let's dive into this together. Let's explore how we can embrace our bustling brains and eat healthy.

Did I say stay active? LOL!! Nope, not at all, today we are simply discussing how to eat healthy. I'm still developing the active element. Yet, feeling good about us, both internally and externally, is crucial. That's the area where you can join me.

> *"My workout routine comprises running late and lifting my grocery bags—what a workout, right?"*

MY MIRACLE MACHINE

Did you know God is like, **super** smart? I mean, we all know He's God and embodies *ultimate intelligence*—He literally is the definition of wisdom! Who else could command the sun to shine exactly when and where it needs to? Ever wonder who could create the moon and position it so perfectly that every galaxy gets a front-row seat to its breathtaking beauty? That is the same God who designed your body with a remarkable system that circulates blood every 13 seconds, tirelessly working to cleanse out germs and keep you healthy.

How amazing is that?

I always struggled with my self-image and health, feeling disconnected from my body. One day, I discovered something excellent about myself and learned an essential truth: He created my body, my "Miracle Machine"! He knows every part of me. Who better to be right alongside me on my health adventure than God?

Realizing that overcoming health challenges wasn't solely dependent on *my* strength came to me after this revelation. It was about being in communion with Him, making daily decisions with His guidance. I incorporated more fresh fruits, veggies, and leafy greens into my diet, recognizing that He knew what He was doing when He created these natural foods to fuel our bodies.

> *What if we could blend our hectic minds with a wellness regimen that doesn't seem burdensome? Kind of, like eating a salad on a trampoline. Bouncing towards health sounds more fun, right?"*

At first glance, this might seem like a boring life–always in a hurry to spend time with people, and to eat lettuce with apples. Not me! I want fun food, fast food, but make it healthy. You may think that's impossible, but I am proof that it isn't. I do not need steaks or French fries to keep me going; I need fuel that's good for my body. The key to success is learning how to incorporate the macronutrients your body requires sustaining your metabolism.

GAINING MOMENTUM

My journey towards healthier living gained momentum when I started planning my meals and habits with my friends and family. We embraced the wisdom of Proverbs 21:5: "Good planning and hard work lead to prosperity, but hasty shortcuts lead to poverty." Together, we focused on creating attainable goals and realistic meal plans.

One of our favorite activities was making smoothies, a delightful blend of God's creations. Smoothies became our go-to fast food, filled with nourishing ingredients that energized our bodies and souls. For breakfast, I love a hearty plate with scrambled eggs, avocado toast, and a side of fresh berries. Lunch often features a vibrant salad with mixed greens, grilled chicken, and a sprinkle of nuts and seeds. Dinner? We do not worry about it until dinnertime. Let's attempt to dissipate all the built-up energy while stressing over things of the future. Make a stand today to keep the main thing the main thing.

In the struggle for healthy lifestyles in a fast-paced world, the main thing is to **stop stressing** over it being too hard or unattainable. If God is concerned about what goes into your mouth, *it is attainable*. Just like salvation, you must start seeing yourself differently, then walk out the different you that you are becoming.

Embrace the journey with faith and intention, knowing that with God's guidance and a little planning, a healthier you are not just a dream, but a divine and absolute possibility.

MADE IN HIS IMAGE

For years, I prayed fervently for God to connect me with a community where I could share my health journey and inspire others facing similar struggles. And let me tell you, when God responded to that prayer, it was like finding the secret ingredient in my favorite smoothie! We launched a group at church called "Beautiful," and did we strike gold!

At our initial "Beautiful" event, excitement buzzed like a blender on high as we dove into crafting a delightful array of smoothies. Picture this: Chocolate Coffee Protein Shakes that make you feel like a superhero and refreshing Vanilla Orange Smoothies that scream summer vibes! We mixed, whipped, and sipped our way to healthier habits, all while enjoying the deliciousness and camaraderie. Who knew healthy could taste this good?

As I embrace these fresh routines, I am also nurturing my soul. My physical body might age like a fine wine, but my spirit? It is more like vintage cheese—getting better with age! Scriptures like Habakkuk 2:2 remind me to have a clearly defined vision. Each week, I boldly declare a powerful confession: "I am as bold as a lion! With You as my strength and shield, I can endure to the end. I possess the capacity for victorious living, operating in excellence and purpose to complete every task I set out to do. Through Christ who gives me strength, I can do all things." Talk about a pep talk!

You may wonder why my story is so important. If you have ever walked—whether for a week or even just a day—at 370 pounds through malls, restaurants, crowded stores, or doctor's offices, you would never question its significance. You would know firsthand the ridicule and judgment that can make you feel you are carrying not just your weight, but the weight of the world on your shoulders. And trust me, this journey has more layers than a triple-decker cake—so much more to share, but that is a story for another day.

Today, I want to focus on the weight loss journey, the part you can see with your own eyes. I stand before you, giving God all the glory for these 200-pounds I have shed.

Without Him, I would never have made it to this page.

We can see that faith, determination, and perhaps a little divine intervention prove that anything is possible—even lifting the heaviest burdens. So, let us lift our spirits and celebrate this journey together!

Sharing my journey, I encourage others to set achievable goals, create meal plans, and choose simple, nutritious foods. My story resonated deeply, inspiring many to embark on their own healthy adventures, reassured by the knowledge that they were not alone. They had Him by their side, guiding them every step of the way.

Together, we are thriving, discovering beauty in our bodies and souls, and living our days with joy and purpose. You too can experience this transformation, through Smoothies and God.

Inner peace is essential, but it's not enough; you must also navigate the external world's challenges. Embracing your true self, flaws and all, is crucial for success in today's world. The Spirit's power, driven by God's eternal mission, resonates through all beings, guiding and empowering us. It's not enough to just survive in your world; you must acknowledge the inner Christ and confidently step into the calling(s) and purpose(s) He has given you, feeling the powerful presence that guides.

"Just remember, the only thing that should bust out is our confidence!"

Notes

Chapter 3 | He Will Lead

If we could grasp that one thing. Fill in the blank with your name _____ (insert your name here), a (what is your calling) _____ (You the Apostle, Prophetess, Pastor, Evangelist, Leader, Laborer, Visionary, is making positive change and trusting that He will lead.

We must fine-tune the call we feel deep within. The key lies in discovering your true self and embracing the gifts God has placed inside you without fear. Unearthing this calling is not just a journey; it's an awakening. Are you ready to step into the fullness of your divine purpose? — sent not from men nor by a man, but by Jesus Christ and God the Father. You were called, gifted, and sent out by Father and Son, filled with Holy Spirit to do great and mighty works. If love guides you, nothing can stop you.

A calling not of human origin, but Holy. God uniquely chose you, equipping you with spiritual gifts and anointing you to make an impact.

I believe: Each possesses a sphere of influence. It is imperative that you be the Lookers for your sphere. If nothing else, ensure that you are standing guard for those God trusts you with!

> *"And the Lord was going before them in a pillar of cloud by day to lead them on the way, and in a pillar of fire by night to give them light, so that they might travel by day and by night." (Exodus 13:21 NASB2020)*

The Lord guided the Israelites from the Exodus to the Promised Land. A cloud led them during the day, and a fire led them at night. God is just as faithful to us if we allow Him to lead. Admitting our inability to do it without Him is the first step in experiencing His divine guidance.

Nehemiah 6 showcases his determination and wisdom when facing opposition. In verse 3, he boldly dismisses his enemies' attempts to distract and intimidate him, saying, "I am doing a great work and cannot come down. Why should the work stop while I leave it and come down to you?"

This verse highlights the importance of staying focused on God's work, despite external pressures and distractions. It shows the power of purpose and the need to prioritize God's mission over the schemes of those who try to undermine it. Nehemiah's unwavering resolve reminds us to remain dedicated to fulfilling God's calling, no matter the opposition.

Discernment is *vital*. Understanding that you are on assignment from God is *key*. Feel the boldness rise within you, speak against the enemy's tactics with unwavering courage, and *refuse* to be shaken. This boldness will propel you to the next level.

In this story, Nehemiah faced daunting challenges. The words of doubt and fear reached him and shook him. Yet, he knew he was on assignment from God and prayed for strength. Nehemiah prayed for God to strengthen *his* hands. He recognized that his mission was divine and that ultimately, God *would see him through.*

Tonia Mierez's Story: A Testimony of God's Guidance

There was a time in my life when everything seemed to fall apart. The weight of life's challenges was heavy, and the path forward was unclear. As a woman of faith, I found this season testing my beliefs in ways I had never experienced before.

One evening, after a tough day, I found myself alone in my room, tears streaming down my face. I felt lost and overwhelmed, struggling with my self-worth and purpose. In that moment of despair, I reached out to God with all my heart, praying for guidance and strength.

These moments when you don't know what to do, if God hears you or if it is all just a figment of your imagination. This was one of those days where the struggle to muster faith was screaming in my face.

As I prayed, a sense of peace washed over me. It was as if a warm light was filling the room, lifting the heaviness from my heart. I felt a gentle prompting in my spirit, a quiet whisper that says, "Trust *Me*. I have a plan." This was true peace that passes all understanding.

Inspired by my encounter with Holy Spirit, I took a step of faith. He inspired me to create a "Beautiful" class, designed to enrich women's lives. This class was designed to help women discover the hidden places in their hearts, understanding that true beauty comes from within. But more than that, finding themselves in Him is the most powerful thing I have ever experienced.

To my surprise, over 50 people signed up for the class initially. However, the first session saw only 32 attendees. This left me with questions, wondering why the other 20 who registered did not attend. Some of these never engaged in the class, and I told myself that they might have had the initial desire but were struggling with walking into the room. I too have had moments where walking into the room was simply more that I could attain. Others came for the first three weeks, but their enthusiasm waned by the fourth week.

During one session in June, something remarkable happened. We felt an incredible sense of unity and purpose. The connection and support we experienced went beyond just numbers; it filled the atmosphere.

The powerful session resonated deeply, and in the following two months, a wave of positive change washed over many lives, clear in their renewed energy and focus. We could see it in their faces and posture. The ladies began to commune with God on a deeper level and we watched as they began to emerge from inside themselves. I saw many transformations from this small group that still resonates loudly today.

Many testimonies emerged from this group, with some women coming out of deep depression. Holy Spirit renewed hearts and souls.

Picture a community where beauty's value is paramount. Where the community shares and celebrates every story, struggle, and triumph. I would love to help you set up a Beautiful group in your own community.

Join us and be part of something amazing. Your journey of self-discovery and empowerment is waiting. Let's create something beautiful together.

His Plan Was Crystal Clear

He fulfilled the goal He set for this ministry. Before we even began, He gave me a coherent plan...

EMBRACE AUTHENTICITY

God instructed me to show the ladies that being true to oneself is acceptable. He urged me to stop hiding and be real with them. This was not about being fake, but about being fully present.

DELIVER TWELVE LESSONS

He guided me to teach twelve lessons clearly, assuring me He would bring the right people to each session. My task was simply to be faithful and not worry about the details.

Host Three Key Events

- Bonding and learning about healthy eating will be fun with a smoothie night!
- We invited a small group of ladies to a pool party to foster deeper connections.
- Having a shopping day is a way to support prudent spending and sound financial habits, as guided by God's word. Not to mention great coffee, food and a party dress try-on party... That was the best!

Plan a Makeup Party

In the first week, God inspired me to organize a makeup party for fun and bonding. He intended to reveal someone's secret; I only discovered their identity later. More details on this will follow later in the book.

He also instructed me while I was teaching the first night to create monthly Buddies. This came straight out of my spirit, flowed up my vocal cords into my mouth and out into the airwaves like an unstoppable force. God wanted to say something and there was nothing I could do to hold it back.

God works well through plans.

GOALS FOR THE WEEK

Seek Guidance:

For a successful weight loss journey, find time for daily prayer and meditation, seeking strength and guidance from the Lord. Lay hands on the part(s) of your body that bothers you most. Over your body, speak the Word of God. Command your body to line up to the Word and speak to your Spirit. Remind yourself that you are a daughter of the King and that nothing with your Daddy is impossible.

Establish Healthy Eating Habits:

Eat more fruits, vegetables, and whole grains. Cut down on processed and unhealthy foods. Focus on a diet that's high in protein and low in calories.

Physical Activity:

Daily, aim for 5-30 minutes of moderate exercise, such as shaking, wall Pilates, chair Pilates, walking, jogging, or a workout guided by the Lord's strength.

Accountability:

Find an accountability partner, a "buddy". Share with this person things about yourself and work together to find God's happy place for you. After finding an accountability partner, schedule a phone call to share your weight loss goals. Discuss your successes and your faith in your ability to improve. Remember: failure doesn't exist.

Trust in the Lord:

Achieving your weight loss goals will result from remembering your dependence on God's guidance and strength daily. Since His help make all things possible, surrender your struggles and weaknesses to Him.

THIS WEEK'S CONFESSION

Throughout this week, I boldly declare my commitment to walk in Your divine presence, O God, honoring You in every aspect of my life, including my dietary choices. I humbly surrender my weight, health, and body to Your care and guidance. With unwavering courage, disciplined resolve, and steadfast perseverance, I confront each test and temptation that comes my way. In You, I am abundantly blessed, prosperous, and destined for triumphant success.

> *"The Lord went ahead of them. He guided them during the day with a pillar of cloud, and he provided light at night with a pillar of fire. This allowed them to travel by day or by night. And the Lord did not remove the pillar of cloud or pillar of fire from its place in front of the people." _ (Exodus 13:21-22 NASB2020)*

Remember, in the fire, He is there. In the storm, He is there. He will never walk away from us, and He will always lead us to victory, just as He did for Tonia Mierez and countless others who trust in

His guidance. He will also lead you exactly where you need to be.

He Will Lead

> *And the LORD went before them by day in a pillar of a cloud to lead them the way; and by night in a pillar of fire, to give them light; to go by day and night. (Exodus 13:21 KJV)*

"God guided them like a fleet of adventure drones, using a cloud during the day and a fire at night, charting their course and lighting their path so they could embark on their journey with confidence and excitement, traveling safely at all times."

Admitting to him your inability to do it without him? Giving yourself the permission to trust?

"From the exodus to their arrival in the Promised Land, the Israelites were guided by His divine guidance. This serves as a powerful reminder that when we allow God to lead us, His unwavering faithfulness lights our path, even through the most challenging journeys."

Life often presents us with overwhelming challenges and uncertainties. As the Israelites relied on God's guidance during their desert journey, so we can trust in His leadership for our daily challenges. By admitting our inability to navigate life's complexities without Him, we open ourselves to His divine guidance and support.

Remember, God's presence is constant, whether we are in moments of clarity or in the darkest of nights. He is there to lead us, to light our path, and to provide the strength we need to keep. Trust in His faithfulness and let Him be your guide.

MY PLANS ARE NOT ALWAYS GOD'S PLANS

Initially, I had hoped for a small group of up to twenty to keep the setting intimate, allowing for personal growth and togetherness. The more people you host in a group atmosphere, the less personal it becomes. Yet I am overjoyed with God's pathway. If He wants thousands, we shall proclaim His goodness on the housetops. But if He wants two, we will sit with coffee mugs and chat on the sofa.

Holy Spirit has guided me since my early teens and still leads me today. He called me into youth pastoral ministries, leading to my role as associate pastor at Cupbearer Ministry Church in Dunlap, TN. God then guided me to The Lord's House in Dalton, GA, as an outreach pastor, where I had the privilege of leading and serving with many passionate evangelists and devoted followers of the Jesus.

Later, I took a season of rest at Casey Treat's ministry in Seattle, Washington. There, I experienced *true love* in ministry and learned the importance of discipleship, making it part of every ministry I engage in. After that, Holy Spirit led me back to Northwest Christian Fellowship, where I led praise and worship for a few years. During this time, I had profound moments with Holy Spirit, affecting the lives of incredible people and forming lifelong friendships, especially with my husband, David Mierez, and my lifelong friend, Beverly Gibson Sherman.

Sometimes we overlook our own selves and forget to realize that God's plan includes us too. We must take some time and realize that He is making us, He is molding us and He is guiding our every step. It's time for us to acknowledge the journey.

IS SPIRITUAL DEPRESSION REAL?

In 2011, my husband and I entered a ten-year spiritual depression, during which we wandered, cried, and prayed for God's guidance to show us what was wrong and how to change things. The anguish we felt during this time is unexplainable and would take the whole book to paint the picture. I will cut to the end... In 2023, we visited a revitalized church in Dalton, GA, called Lifegate. We birthed the Beautiful Group here. We are now eagerly awaiting to see where God leads us next, confident that He will anoint the path we take.

Throughout this journey, I have witnessed God's hand at work in countless ways. While many believe that reaching people in large numbers is the most impactful approach, I have learned that sometimes God's work is best accomplished through intimate settings and one-on-one interactions. His ways are always higher than our own, so we should never confine Him to our limited perspectives.

We will dig into spiritual depression, in the next chapter...

Chapter 4 | Prayer Only Refuse Worry

You know what they tell you about worrying and frown lines? Ohhhh and we DO NOT want those pesky things! Be gone worry! Be gone wrinkles!

Jesus asked the disciples to pray so that they would not fall into temptation (Luke 22:40). He anticipated many challenges and wanted them to take the initiative. After Jesus instructed them, he then walked away from them and prayed on his own. As he prayed, verse 43 says that "an angel from heaven appeared and strengthened him."

Spiritual Depression | Let's Talk About It...

I sought the Lord, and He

heard, and He answered!

That is why I trust Him!

As mentioned in chapter 3, spiritual depression can have a profound impact on various aspects of your life. It is a silent thief that robs you of your purpose, joy, and spiritual connection. We struggled for many years, lost in the shadows of despair, unaware of what had a grip on us. Until approximately three months before we found deliverance, I had never heard of such a thing. If someone had mentioned the term to me back then, I probably would have dismissed it as ridiculous, unable to comprehend the deep, pervasive impact it was having on our lives.

Spiritual depression will leave you feeling disconnected from your faith, purposeless, and emotionally drained. It can make you question your beliefs, your worth, and your path. It was not until we were on the brink of breaking that we found the light of deliverance, a light that revealed the profound depth of our spiritual struggle and the strength we never knew we had.

This journey taught us that recognizing and addressing spiritual depression is crucial for regaining your spiritual health and vitality. It's about understanding that you are not alone, there is hope, and through faith in God (Yahweh), support, and resilience, you can overcome even the deepest spiritual struggles.

Here are the key areas that it can affect:

Sense of Purpose

Loss of Direction: Individuals may feel a lack of purpose or meaning in their spiritual journey, leading to confusion and disorientation.

Connection with Faith

Disconnection: There can be a feeling of being distant from your faith or beliefs, which might cause decreased participation in spiritual practices like prayer, worship, or meditation.

Emotional Well-being

Despair and sadness: Spiritual depression often brings about deep feelings of sadness, hopelessness, and despair.

Increased Anxiety: Your spiritual state and worries of the future may heighten your anxiety.

Motivation and Enthusiasm

Reduced Motivation: Individuals may struggle with a lack of motivation to engage in activities they once found fulfilling and joyful.

Diminished Enthusiasm: The joy and enthusiasm that usually accompany spiritual practices and community involvement can vanish.

Social Relationships

Isolation: People might withdraw from their spiritual community, friends, and family, leading to feelings of isolation and loneliness.

Strained Relationships: Spiritual struggles can strain personal relationships, especially if loved ones do not understand what the person is going through.

Self-Identity

Crisis of identity: There can be a sense of confusion about your identity and worth, leading to self-doubt and loss of self-esteem.

Spiritual Crisis: If you question your beliefs and values, this can cause a crisis of faith, profoundly challenging your previously held convictions.

Physical Health

Fatigue: The emotional toll of spiritual depression can manifest physically, leading to fatigue and other health issues.

Neglected Self-care: Individuals may neglect self-care practices, resulting in a decline in overall physical health.

Hope and Future Outlook

Hopelessness: A pervasive sense of hopelessness can make it difficult to look forward to the future or believe that things will improve.

Lack of vision impairs the ability to envision a positive and fulfilling future.

Coping and Healing

Addressing spiritual depression means seeking support, engaging in spiritual practices that resonate with you, and connecting with a supportive community. It's important to acknowledge these feelings and take steps towards healing. Things like talking to a trusted spiritual advisor, joining a faith-based support group, or rekindling your faith and purpose.

Remember, spiritual depression is a journey, and with the right support and resources, individuals can find their way back to a place of hope and spiritual renewal.

Spiritual depression refers to a state where an individual experiences a deep sense of sadness, emptiness, or disconnection, specifically related to their spiritual life. It's different from clinical depression, though they can share some similar symptoms. Here are the key aspects of spiritual depression:

Symptoms of Spiritual Depression

For me, I did not want to leave my house. The side effects of this level of depression cause much stress, anxiety, and for me, weight gain. My husband went through a very dark season that I will let him tell you about when he is ready to share.

Loss of Connection: Feeling disconnected from your faith, spiritual practices, or community.

Doubt and Uncertainty: Struggling with doubts about your beliefs or the meaning of life.

Lack of purpose: Feeling a sense of purposelessness or questioning the significance of your spiritual journey.

Emotional Struggles: Experiencing feelings of guilt, shame, or worthlessness related to spiritual beliefs.

Withdrawal: Avoiding spiritual practices, worship, or fellowship because of a sense of unworthiness or disinterest.

Causes of Spiritual Depression

Life Crises: Major life events such as loss, illness, or trauma can trigger spiritual doubts and emotional struggles.

Unresolved Sin or guilt: Feeling burdened by unresolved sins or guilt can lead to a sense of spiritual alienation.

Lack of Community Support: A weak or non-supportive spiritual community can exacerbate feelings of isolation and despair.

Perceived Distance from God: Feeling that God is distant or unresponsive can lead to a deep sense of spiritual loneliness.

COPING WITH SPIRITUAL DEPRESSION

Seek Support: Talk to a trusted spiritual advisor, pastor, or counselor who can provide guidance and support. Do not wait another day! Contact someone today to help you get through this season. We will talk about seasons in the next book.

Engage in prayer: Pray even when you do not think they are getting through the ceiling. These practices can help re-establish a connection with your faith and provide comfort.

Join a Faith Community: Go to worship, somewhere, with someone or alone if you must. Being part of a supportive community can offer encouragement and a sense of belonging.

Reflect and Journal: Writing about your feelings and experiences can help process emotions and gain clarity.

Focus on Scripture: "Don't just read the Word, 'Read' the Word."

Dig Deeper! Reading and reflecting on scriptures that speak of hope, love, and God's presence can be reassuring.

HEALING AND HOPE

Spiritual depression, like any form of depression, can be challenging to navigate. But it is important to remember that help is available, and recovery is possible. Seeking support, engaging in spiritual practices, and allowing oneself to process and reflect can lead to healing and renewed faith.

The Bible addresses feelings of despair, hopelessness, and spiritual struggle in various passages. While it might not use the exact term "spiritual depression," the themes and guidance provided can offer comfort and insight for those experiencing such feelings. Here are a few key points:

Passages Addressing Despair and Hope

Psalm 42:11:

Why, my soul, are you downcast? Why so disturbed within me? Put your hope in God, for I will yet praise him, my Savior, and my God.

This verse acknowledges feelings of being downcast (spiritually depressed) and encourages placing hope in God.

Psalm 34:17-18:

The righteous cry out, and the Lord hears them; he delivers them from all their troubles. The Lord draws near to the brokenhearted and rescues those crushed in spirit.

These verses emphasize God hears and is close to those who are brokenhearted and in distress.

Matthew 11:28-30:

> *Come to me, all you who are weary and burdened, and I will give you rest. Take my yoke upon you and learn from me, for I am gentle and humble in heart, and you will find rest for your souls. For my yoke is easy and my burden is light.*

Jesus invites those who are weary to come to Him for rest and relief from their burdens.

> *Philippians 4:6-7:*

> *Do not be anxious about anything, but in every situation, by prayer and petition, with thanksgiving, present your requests to God. And the peace of God, which transcends all understanding, will guard your hearts and your minds in Christ Jesus.*

These verses encourage prayer and reliance on God's peace to ease anxiety and distress. Reading them are not enough, you must immerse yourself in them, eat them like chocolate and allow ourself to become consumed with the healing power that exists.

Examples of Spiritual Depression in Biblical Figures

- Elijah: In 1 Kings 19, Elijah experiences deep despair and exhaustion after fleeing from Queen Jezebel. He

feels alone and wishes to die, but God provides for him, sends an angel to comfort him, and ultimately renews his strength and purpose.
- David: Many of David's psalms show his struggles with feelings of despair and his reliance on God for strength and comfort.
- Job: Job's story is a profound exploration of suffering, where he experiences deep anguish but ultimately finds restoration and deeper faith.

Encouragement and Comfort

Isaiah 41:10:

So, do not fear because I am with you. I will strengthen you and help you; I will uphold you with my righteous right hand.

This verse offers reassurance of God's presence and support.

How To Actually Do It

- Seek God in prayer: Express your feelings to God and seek His guidance and comfort.
- Meditate on Scripture: Reflect on verses that speak of God's love, support, and promises.
  - Have any sticky notes? If not use a tube of lipstick and get these verses on your bathroom mirror. Read them each time you look at yourself and remember to slow your

> - brain down long enough to hear what you are reading.
>   - Read them out loud and listen to the words.
> - Community Support: Surround yourself with a supportive faith community that can provide encouragement and prayer.

"I was raised to keep things to myself, to not let anyone know what's going on, and to stay strong through the pain. While I still follow this to some extent, I've learned that when I'm struggling, it's okay to raise a white flag and reach out to those who can help lift me back up."

Goals For the Week

Daily Prayer

Dedicate time each day for prayer, seeking strength and guidance from the Lord to overcome temptation and worries.

Refusal of Worry

Commit to refusing worry and anxiety by surrendering them to God in prayer whenever they arise.

Nourishing Nutrition

Strive to nourish the body with wholesome nutrition each day, making mindful choices that honor God's gift of health.

Bold Requesting

Boldly present requests to the Lord, believing in His power to exceed expectations and manifest blessings beyond measure. (I know He can take away the calories, but is this really a wise move? Use that miracle for something will power cannot consume. Eat one or two bites instead of the whole thing).

Strength in Solitude

Follow Jesus' example by spending solitary time in prayer, allowing God to strengthen and empower in times of need. (Go to the closet for 10 minutes... take a bath and enjoy "me" time with God).

This Weeks Confession

My worries and anxieties vanish thanks to my faith, and I'm grateful for access to nutritious food. Because my heart overflows with thankfulness, I boldly present my requests to You, O Lord.

By passionately believing in Your omnipotent ability to manifest them beyond measure, I exceed even my loftiest expectations.

He told them there to pray against succumbing to temptation.

By letting God's essence permeate our lives, we develop the capacity to shun anything that disrupts the harmony of our world.

Chapter 5 | Validation Vortex

Co-Authored by Haley Mooney

— Consequences...

HARD COLD FACTS...

There I was, standing in front of the mirror, squinting at my reflection like it held the answers to the universe. Did I still "have it"? Was I still a contender in the never-ending beauty pageant that life seems to be? Society whispers its relentless demands, and I am stuck with the consequences. The never-ending comparison to others, the low self-esteem. That I will never live up to what the world expects of me. Society says, "You should have enormous eyes and a big butt. You should have a small waist, but don't be too skinny. Have some meat on you, but don't be fat. Your nose should be cute, and your lips should be plump. You should have a nice chest, and your legs should look nice in a dress. Your skin should be flawless. No lines, wrinkles, or acne scars. No stretch marks or imperfections of any kind. Anything less is unacceptable."

At some point we must stop the constant tug-of-war.

I believed for a long time that I needed to meet every one of these expectations. I entangled my self-worth with the fleeting glances of approval from others, the casual compliments about my appearance, and the rare, yet oh-so-sweet, head-turns on the street. You know what I am talking about—the moments when a certain someone's eyes light up just a little too brightly when they see you. Whoop! Did I just say something?

Yes, I did. I, like many of us, sought validation from every angle: mirrors, others' words, gestures, and eye contact from certain individuals on certain days to ensure that I still "had it." It is exhausting, isn't it? This constant need to confirm our worthiness, to measure up to this arbitrary standard set by people who don't know us, and frankly, don't care about our well-being.

God wants to show you...

Let us talk about the consequences of living in this validation vortex. For me, it led to burnout. I was constantly striving to meet everyone's expectations—my boss's, my friends, even strangers. I spent hours on beauty treatments, tried every diet known to humankind, and bought more clothes than I care to admit, all in the name of being "enough." But it was never enough. The more I tried to please, the emptier I felt. My self-confidence tanked, leaving me feeling like a shell of the person I wanted to be.

I remember a time when my need for approval hit an all-time high. I was at a party, feeling fabulous in my new dress. As the night went on, I realized I was spending more time worrying about who was looking at me and what they were thinking than enjoying myself. It was a wake-up call. My obsession with external validation was robbing me of genuine joy and connection.

Understanding Your Worth

I came to understand, through prayer, support, and Holy Spirit, that my worth is not determined by my appearance or others' approval. It comes from being a child of God, created in His image. This realization was freeing. It allowed me to set boundaries, prioritize my relationship with God, and focus on what mattered.

So, if you seek validation from all the wrong places, remember this: you are already enough. You do not need the world's approval to be beautiful. Embrace who you are, flaws and all, and let God's love be the source of your confidence. It is a journey, but with each step, you'll find that you're not just a conqueror—you're a beacon of God's glory.

One thing we must do is make a positive choice to release the hold that others have on us to please. Without moving beyond this station in life, we face consequences. This journey requires that we confront the expectations and pressures placed upon us and courageously embrace our true identities, unshackled from the need for external validation.

As women, we often fall into the trap of trying to please others instead of God. Society determines our value based on our appearance, career success, social status, and family roles. However, these efforts can lead to burnout, a sense of emptiness, and even mental health issues such as anxiety and depression. When we strive to meet the world's expectations, we risk losing sight of our true purpose and the unique calling God has for us.

LIFE STORIES FROM INCREDIBLE WOMEN...

Imagine adding your story to this Hall of Fame. What would your chapter reveal?

Weight Loss Struggles from Woman #2

Consider me, who struggled with weight for most of my life. The pressure to conform to society's standards of beauty, equating thinness with worthiness, was immense. I tried countless diets and extreme exercise regimens, but nothing seemed to work. I always ended up defeated and feeling unattractive, believing I could never be beautiful unless I lost weight. My turning point came when I started on the last journey to lose weight. Understanding the call of God in my life gave me something I never had before, a correct view of my worth. I saw myself differently. I focused on health rather than appearance, embracing a balanced lifestyle. Gradually, I am losing the weight, but more importantly, I am constantly gaining confidence and a deeper understanding of my identity in Christ.

The Pleaser - Woman #3

Consider me, who always sought to please my colleagues and friends by taking on extra work and always being available. I thought this would make me more valuable and appreciated. But this left me exhausted and resentful, with little time for family or personal growth. I realized my need to please others stemmed from a desire for acceptance and validation only God could provide. I set boundaries, prioritize my relationship with God, and focus on the values that mattered to me. There is so much more to this story, but we will save it for another time.

Validate Me now! Woman #4

Consider me, who always sought the validation of men, even if it damaged me. I have always had a desire for love. To be loved and to love. At this point in my life, I had incredibly low self-esteem, and I did not value myself as a person, so I sought validation elsewhere. Having a man tell me how beautiful my face and body were, it was, for lack of better words, addicting. This leads me down a rabbit hole of selling myself to men online. Degrading myself because it made a man happy, and by making the man happy, it made me happy. But it never lasted. They often blocked or removed me the next day. I felt empty and used. I was a toy to be played with and discarded. My problem? I was looking for love in places where love didn't exist. I needed God to tell me I didn't deserve to be degraded and treated like a toy. My beauty didn't depend on a man's approval. I was already beautiful in my creator's eyes.

Submission or subjugation? Woman #5

Imagine me, a woman who grew up in the care of my grandmother. Seeing her hold the Bible, her weapon of choice, would send shivers down my spine. An echo filled the room: the sound of its pages turning, carrying a sense of impending judgment. The smell of old leather and musty paper wafted from its worn cover, intensifying the weight of its authority. Her words lingered in every interaction, etching shame and humiliation into my very being. I was often terrified of stepping into church for fear of being outcaste and disapproved of. I tried my best to conform to what I thought the "churchgoers" wanted of me. This led to me often shutting everyone out and creating a mask to hide who I truly was. I ended up leaving the church altogether, as I was tired of the judgment. I ended up getting involved in terrible stuff with some bad people. Attending my current church recently made me realize I never needed the approval of others. I had the approval and love of my Father.

Starved for Attention - Woman #6

Consider me, someone who was chronically on social media. I followed many models and influencers whom the world deemed extremely beautiful. I envied everything about them, from their small and petite figure to their big eyes and long, luscious hair. They seemed to look beautiful in everything they wore, even if the item itself was ugly. Self-consciousness and my appearance became a significant concern for me. I hated looking in the mirror because I knew I'd never look like the women I saw online. My return to God began one night when I encountered Psalm 139:13-14. I realized I didn't need to look like anyone else as I was, fearfully and wonderfully made.

We often feel as if we are alone in our struggles. But there are thousands, if not millions, of stories like these. The world has placed the need for validation from others into the minds of so many women. We don't need the world's flawed validation; we need God's graceful and eternal love, which we didn't need to break ourselves for.

Other Things That Make Us Feel Less Beautiful by the World's Sentiment:

1. Women often feel a constant weight on their shoulders, as if they are standing on a never-ending treadmill.
    a. Witnessing: Watching colleagues ascend the corporate ladder, their success echoing around them, can feel like a constant, piercing gaze. The sound of typing keyboards reverberates through the office, a symphony of ambition and determination. The air

carries a faint scent of stress and anxiety, intertwining with the aroma of freshly brewed coffee.
b. Career Pressures: With every passing day, the pressure mounts, causing their hearts to race and their palms to grow clammy. The feeling of inadequacy lingers in their minds, like a heavy fog that obscures their confidence.

2. **Social Media Comparison**: The curated (made up sometimes and there we see what everyone wants us to see) lives of others on social media can create unrealistic standards. Constantly comparing ourselves to the perfect lives of others can erode our self-esteem and make us feel less beautiful and less accomplished.

3. **Family Expectations**: The pressure to be the perfect mother, wife, or daughter can be overwhelming. Trying to meet all the expectations of family roles can leave us feeling like we are never enough, diminishing our sense of self-worth.

MOVING BEYOND THE STRUGGLE:

- **Identify the Triggers**: Reflect on situations where you feel the need to please others. Is it in your workplace, social gatherings, or even at home?

- **Seek God's Approval**: Meditate on scriptures that affirm your identity in Christ and remind you that God's approval matters most.

- **Set Boundaries**: Learn to say no to commitments that do not align with your values or drain your energy. Prioritize activities that nourish your soul and strengthen your relationship with God.

- **Cultivate Inner Beauty**: Focus on developing qualities like kindness, patience, and humility, which are pleasing to God and show His character.

- **Pray for Transformation**: Ask God to help you release the need to please others and transform your heart to seek His will above all else.

CONSEQUENCES OF NOT MOVING BEYOND:

- **Burnout**: Constantly trying to please others can lead to physical and emotional exhaustion.

- **Loss of identity**: You may lose sight of who you truly are, and the unique purpose God has for your life.

- **Strained Relationships**: Over-committing to please others can lead to neglecting important relationships, including your relationship with God.

- **Spiritual Stagnation**: Focusing on worldly approval can hinder your spiritual growth and prevent you from experiencing the fullness of life God offers.

Just Faith - Never Failure:

Take the first step in faith. You do not have to see the whole staircase, just take the first step. ~ Martin Luther King Jr.

In choosing to break free from the need to please others, we step into the fullness of the life God intended for us. It is a journey of faith, where we learn to trust in His promises and embrace our unique calling.

I will not be conformed to this world, but I will be changed by the renewal of my mind!

Offer your body as a living sacrifice, holy and acceptable and pleasing to Him.

God wants to show you your next steps more than you want to see them.

GOALS FOR THE WEEK

- Reflect on areas where you feel pressured to meet others' expectations.

- Meditate on scriptures that affirm your identity in Christ.

- Take practical steps to prioritize God's view over societal standards.

THIS WEEK'S CONFESSION

My heart overflows with thankfulness for your steadfast commitments. Every day, I press hard forward, moving from triumph to triumph, from success to success, growing stronger with every step. I am not merely a conqueror; I am a force. In every endeavor, I forge ahead, unstoppable, and unwavering in my pursuit of greatness.

> "I will drive them out a little at a time until your population has increased enough to take possession of the land." (Exodus 23:30, GW)

> "Little by little, I will force them out of your way until you have increased enough to take possession of the land." (Exodus 23:30, NLT)

Remember, the transformation of your life begins with a single step of faith. Embrace who God created you to be and let go of the need to conform to the world's expectations. Your journey is unique, and your impact will be profound. You are not just a conqueror; you are a beacon of God's glory.

ABOUT OUR CO-AUTHOR

Allow me to share a brief insight into the essence of our co-author, Hailee Mooney. Amidst the storm, I witnessed the true beauty of nature unfold before my eyes. A heart brimming with gentle warmth, resembling a hearth fire during a winter evening, and a soul restless yet prepared to soar. The world witnesses her wings soar as her spirit praises the Father who rescued her from the ashes. Let me just say that she is one to watch, follow and get to know.

The night of the make-up party Holy Spirit began to reveal much to me about this beauty. Without a doubt, God is doing incredible things in Hailee's life, but the full extent of what's coming is still a mystery.

Hailee Mooney

Hailee, stay focused and cherish the wonderful truth that lives within you. Before we even started the group, the Lord revealed something profound to me about you. I could see right away that His hand was guiding your life.

I have witnessed a remarkable transformation in her countenance as the Holy

Spirit visited her, bringing something entirely new. Hailee discovered herself. She saw herself from the inside out, embracing her identity with newfound clarity and confidence.

100% it looks beautiful on her!

Chapter 6 | Slavery to Freedom

Therefore, whether you eat or drink, or whatever you do, do all to the glory of God. 1 Corinthians 10:31

I was once a prisoner, enslaved by the invisible chains of spiritual depression. My mind was a battlefield consumed by darkness and despair. Every day seemed like a battle, with each decision burdened by feelings of guilt and despair. I was in bondage to my body, enslaved by 360 pounds of flesh that lived to choke the life from me. Realizing the necessity of an escape route to freedom, the daunting journey ahead appeared overwhelming.

One morning, amid my deepest sorrow, a ray of hope pierced through the gloom. My friend sent me this resonant scripture: "Do not conform to the pattern of this world but be transformed by the renewing of your mind" (Romans 12:2). It was a call to change, a reminder that God's Word could transform my thoughts. I clung to this promise, believing that renewal was possible.

With newfound determination, I immersed myself in scripture, focused on mind renewal. Each day, I set aside time to meditate on passages that spoke of hope, strength, and God's unyielding love. I reached out to my accountability partner, and together we searched for scriptures that would fortify our spirits. Our FaceTime calls became a lifeline, a space where we could encourage and uplift each other.

As the days turned into weeks, I felt a shift within me. The scriptures took root in my heart, replacing lies with truth and despair with hope. While His words were taking root, my thoughts were transforming, renewed by the life-giving power of God's Word.

IS PRAISE AND WORSHIP A KEY?

My journey to freedom did not end there. I knew I needed to engage in praise and worship actively, celebrating the freedom I had in Christ. Each day, I turned on worship music and lifted my hands in adoration. I danced, I sang, and I poured out my heart to God. In those moments, I felt His presence envelop me, filling me with a profound sense of peace and joy. Worship became a practice session for the freedom I longed to embrace.

Yet, even amid my praise, I remained mindful of my choices. I knew that while I had the freedom to choose, I was not exempt from the consequences of those choices. When I felt tempted to slip back into old patterns, I phoned a friend, prayed, or immersed myself in scripture. I played with my grandbabies, called my kids, and sought to fill my life with positive, life-affirming activities.

TAKING RESPONSIBILITY FOR MY OWN ACTIONS?

Seeking holiness, I committed myself to aligning my actions with God's will. I focused on my heart, mind, will, and emotions, seeking the daily renewal of my spirit. I embraced the journey of transformation with perseverance and dedication, knowing that God's plan for me included both spiritual and physical prosperity.

As I knelt in prayer, I surrendered fully to God's Spirit. I asked Him to govern my thoughts and actions, to lead me into a life of vitality, tranquility, and righteousness. Before each meal, I prayed, seeking His guidance and peace. I became more attuned to my emotions, ensuring that they were in alignment with the Holy Spirit. When my movements felt clumsy and disjointed, I withdrew to find stillness in His presence, praying for renewed harmony and purpose—a sense of calm washed over me.

This journey was arduous, but it was transformative. Each week,

I made a new confession, boldly proclaiming my liberation from the chains of sin:

> *"I courageously decree my independence from the chains of sin. Your unyielding strength and limitless grace have wrought transformation and renewal within me. In You, I embrace a profound shift, journeying towards paths illuminated by holiness and unbounded joy. The life-giving power of Your Spirit has shattered sin's dominion over me. Your Spirit, reigning over my thoughts, infuses me with vitality and serenity, ushering forth a life of profound freedom and fulfillment."*

As I stood before the crowd, the ultimate words of my story echoing in the room, I felt a profound sense of peace. Losing 170 pounds had been a monumental journey, a testament to God's power and grace. My story had become a beacon of hope for so many, living proof that transformation was possible through faith and determination.

I shared how setting realistic goals, crafting meal plans, and choosing easy, nutritious foods had been the key steps in my journey. I spoke of the minor victories and the challenges, but most importantly, I emphasized the unwavering support I had felt from God. It was this divine guidance that had kept me going, even when the path seemed insurmountable.

As I looked into the eyes of those gathered, I could see the flicker of hope and inspiration. My experience had sparked a fire within them, encouraging them to start their own healthy adventures. They understood now that they were never alone; they had Him by their side, guiding them every step of the way.

Together, we thrived, finding beauty in our bodies and souls, and living out our days with joy and purpose. Regardless of your weight or stature, His presence makes you beautiful. Start seeing yourself through His eyes and not your own. Embrace the journey, knowing that with God, transformation and true beauty are always within reach.

CONSCIENTIOUS CHOICES

1. Choice Awareness: Remain mindful of the choices you make throughout the week, recognizing that while you have freedom to choose, you are not exempt from the consequences of those choices.

- When you want to slip, don't do it!

- Phone a friend.

- Pray instead.

- Study instead.

- Play with the kids instead.

- Call the grand-babies.

2. Holiness Pursuit: Commit to living a life guided by paths of holiness and joy, actively seeking to align your actions with God's will and purposes.

- Center your attention to your heart.

- Concentrate on your thoughts.

- Concentrate on your determination.

- Focus on your emotions.

- Keeping all of them aligned with the Father's plan for you. (Spiritual and physical prosperity).

3. Spirit Empowerment: Surrender fully to God's Spirit, allowing Him to govern your thoughts and actions, leading you into a life of vitality, tranquility, and righteousness for the glory of God.

Pray before preparing or eating every meal.

- Focus on your emotions while eating.

- Focus on your peace level. If you sense a disconnect from Holy Spirit, find stillness in His presence to reestablish your alignment.

Do yourself a favor and give "you" time. Nothing worth its salt is a quick process. Understand that time is one of two of the most precious commodities on this planet.

Chapter 7 | Beauty takes time

In our fast-paced world, achieving and maintaining beauty can feel like an endless uphill battle. A barrage of images and standards makes the journey seem overwhelming, but true beauty isn't about fitting into a mold; routines, hard work, and a commitment to self-care that demand time, often mark this paths efforts yet yields profound rewards.

THE POWER OF ROUTINES

Routines are the backbone of our daily lives, and for beauty, they are essential. A consistent skincare regimen, regular exercise, and a balanced diet all play crucial roles in helping us look and feel our best. But establishing these routines is not always easy. It requires discipline and dedication, often in the face of busy schedules and life's unpredictability.

Your *first* priority must be spending time with God. Set aside "your time." My time is 445AM every day. I set my alarm to begin my wake-up time with Him...

The Hard Work Behind the Glow

True beauty is not a passive endeavor. It requires hard work and perseverance. Whether it is pushing through a tough workout, resisting unhealthy temptations, or maintaining a positive mindset amidst challenges, the effort we put in is significant. But with each step, we grow stronger and more resilient, reflecting a beauty that goes beyond the surface.

CONSISTENCY IS KEY

Consistency transforms routines and hard work into lasting results. It is about showing up for us every day, even when it feels difficult. This constancy builds a foundation of self-care that becomes second nature, allowing us to reap the benefits. It is a reminder that beauty is not a fleeting goal but an ongoing journey.

One of the hardest things I have ever done was to willingly show anyone this photo of myself. I am convinced that God's got jokes due to the fact that I was required to also display it for the world to see.

TIME: THE MOST VALUABLE INVESTMENT

The most challenging aspect of self-care is often finding the time. Packed schedules make prioritizing us feel like an impossible task. Yet, taking time for us is crucial. It is in these moments of self-care that we rejuvenate our spirits and enhance our well-being.

A Lighthearted Truth

Oh, no! If I must take time for myself, then I obviously cannot be beautiful. This tongue-in-cheek statement captures the irony we feel. We neglect ourselves in the rush to meet everyone else's needs, thinking that self-care is a luxury we cannot afford. However, it is precisely this time for us that fuels our ability to shine.

Embrace the Journey

The journey to true beauty is not without its struggles. It takes time, effort, and a steadfast commitment to nurturing ourselves. Yet, through these challenges, we discover a deeper, more authentic beauty that radiates from within. By embracing routines, committing to hard work, remaining consistent, and valuing our time, we can transform our lives. Committing to this will show the true beauty that comes from a heart and spirit cared for with love and faith.

This reminds me of the times God has told us to look at His creation and how well He provides and fulfills His promises to them. The myriad instances when God directs our attention to the beauty of nature showcase His influence.

> Remember Matthew 6:28-30 (NIV) "And why do you worry about clothes? See how the flowers of the field grow? They do not labor or spin. Even Solomon, in all his splendor, was not dressed as one of

them. If God so clothes the grass of the field, which is here today and tomorrow is thrown into the fire, **will he not much more** *clothe you—you of little faith?*

Think about the transformation of a butterfly. First, a humble caterpillar, ordinary and insignificant. Through patience and the natural process God designed, it undergoes metamorphosis in a cocoon—a hiding away time. What happens in the hidden times? The waiting, the molding, shaping, and personalization for each one. The "I feel forgotten times." In time, it emerges beautifully, displaying vibrant colors and delicate wings. Just as a butterfly transforms into a stunning creature, God works in our lives, shaping and molding us into the beautiful beings He intends. Trust His process and live during the quiet times, knowing that He cares for you passionately and that He has a plan customized for you.

As we reflect on the transformation process, it is essential to consider our own journeys. What have you learned about yourself during these times of waiting and transformation? How have you grown and changed?

Chapter 8 | Defining Diva Your Way

What have you learned about yourself?

What now? A "diva" originally referred to a celebrated female opera singer, deriving from the Italian word for "goddess." Over time, the term has strengthened to describe any woman with exceptional talent in the performing arts, such as music, theater, or film. However, people often informally use it to describe a demanding, temperamental, or tough woman. The term can carry both positive connotations (showing talent and charisma) and negative ones (showing difficult behavior).

PERSONALLY, I could be both.

Think about how you will let your Diva shine!

A woman can let her "diva" shine by embracing the positive attributes of being driven, inspiring, victorious, and actionable. Here are some ways to do that:

1. DRIVEN

   - Set Clear Goals: Define what you want to achieve and create a plan to reach those goals.

   - Stay Focused: Prioritize tasks and stay dedicated to your ambitions, even when faced with obstacles.

   - Continual Learning: Always seek opportunities to gain experience and grow in your field, enhancing your skills and knowledge.

2. INSPIRING

   - Lead by example: Show integrity, dedication, and positivity in all your actions.

   - Share Your Story: Use your personal journey to motivate and uplift others.

- Support Others: Encourage and mentor those around you, helping them to realize their potential.

Listen: Nothing within you can fathom how much impact you have on the lives of others when you truly take the time to listen to them.

3. VICTORIOUS

- Celebrate Successes: Acknowledge and celebrate your achievements, no matter how small.

- Show resilience by bouncing back from setbacks with grace and determination, proving you can overcome challenges.

- Confidence: Carry yourself with confidence, knowing your worth and abilities.

4. ACTIONABLE

- Take Initiative: Do not wait for opportunities to come to you—create them.

- Be Decisive: Make informed decisions quickly and confidently.

- Follow Through: Ensure you complete what you start, demonstrating reliability and commitment.

By embodying these traits, you can let your "diva" shine in a way that is empowering and uplifting for yourself and those around you.

Beauty Tip: Look in the Mirror

Have you ever wondered what it would be like to trade beauty tips with a Persian queen? Can you imagine the luxurious secrets and timeless tricks she would share? From ancient skincare rituals involving exotic oils and herbs to beauty routines that make you feel like royalty, you would get the royal treatment. Perhaps she would reveal the ancient secret, a whispered family recipe for perfect eyebrows and flawless skin, handed down through generations, its ingredients a closely guarded mystery. With a bit of luck, you could create a signature scent so exquisite, so regal, that even a queen would envy its intoxicating aroma.

Esther's Story

- The book of Esther tells the story of a young Jewish girl who underwent lavish beauty treatments to become the next queen of Persia.

- Esther found favor with King Ahasuerus above all other women and became his bride.

- Despite her pampered life, Esther used her royal position to influence the king and save her people from destruction.

A Lesson for Us All

PREPARATION WITH PURPOSE:

- Just like Esther, we all undergo a time of preparation with a purpose. God uses these periods to shape us for the tasks He has planned.

- Think about it: no one goes through extreme measures to beautify themselves just to stay home. Our beauty, both inner and outer, has a purpose beyond ourselves.

Our Responsibility

Reflecting God's Presence:

- People around us need to feel God and experience His love through our actions and words.

- Before stepping out each day, look in the mirror to check your physical appearance and take a moment to reflect on the Word of God.

Actively apply the Bible's teachings in your life; do not just know them. This inner preparation is essential to show God's beauty and love.

Be a Living Witness

Your Life as a Testament:

- Remember, your life may be the only Bible someone will ever read (2 Corinthians 3:2).

    - Your actions, words, and demeanor should show Christ's love and teachings.

- Embrace your role confidently, knowing that, like Esther, we are all here "for such a time as this" (Esther 4:14, NKJV).

- Unlike Esther, who approached the earthly king without knowing the outcome, we can confidently approach the King of Kings, knowing His promises and His enduring Word.

Practical Application

DAILY REFLECTION:

- Start your day by looking in the mirror and affirming your identity in Christ. Reflect on a scripture that speaks to your heart and declares it over your day.

- Example: "I am fearfully and wonderfully made" (Psalm 139:14).

Engage in Acts of Kindness:

- Seek opportunities to show God's love to others. Whether it is a kind word, a helping hand, or a listening ear, let others feel God's presence through you.

Continuous Learning:

- Commit to regular Bible study and prayer to grow in your understanding and application of God's Word. This will prepare you to be an effective witness in any situation.

Remember that your beauty and confidence come from your identity in Christ and your purpose in His plan. By focusing on others and reflecting on God's love, you can make a profound impact on the world around you.

The following verses contain the story of Esther and the key moments describing her preparation, favor, and influence.

THE PREPARATION OF A QUEEN:

- *Esther 2:8-9. "So it was, when the king's command and decree were heard, and when many young women were gathered at Shushan the citadel, under the custody of Hegai, that Esther also was taken to the king's palace, into the care of Hegai the custodian of the women. Now the young woman pleased him, and she got his favor; so, he readily gave beauty preparations to her, besides her allowance. Then seven choice maidservants were provided for her from the king's palace, and he moved her and her maidservants to the best place in the house of the woman."*

Esther Becomes Queen:

- *Esther 2:17 - "The king loved Esther more than all the other women, and she got grace and favor in his sight more than all the virgins; so, he set the royal crown upon her head and made her queen instead of Vashti."*

A Queenly Influence:

- Esther 4:14-16 - *"For if you remain completely silent at this time, relief and deliverance will arise for the Jews from another place, but you and your father's house will perish. Yet who knows whether you have come to the kingdom for such a time as this?" Then Esther tells them to say to Mordecai: "Go, gather all the Jews who are present in Shushan, and fast for me; neither eat nor drink for three days, night or day. My maids and I will fast likewise. And so, I will go to the king, which is against the law; and if I perish, I perish!"*

Esther Saves Her People:

- Esther 8:3-6 - *"Now Esther spoke again to the king, fell down at his feet, and implored him with tears to counteract the evil of Haman the Agagite, and the scheme which he had devised against the Jews. And the king held out the golden scepter toward Esther. So Esther arose and stood before the king., "If it pleases the king, may he revoke Haman, son of*

Hammedatha the Agagite's letters," she said, "If I have found favor in his sight, and if the thing seems right to him, and if I am pleasing in his eyes, let it be done.". These letters, designed to annihilate the Jews throughout the kingdom, were Haman's doing. For how can I endure to see the evil that will come to my people? Or how can I endure to see the destruction of my countrymen?"

Inspiration from Esther

Esther Arise

- God has need of you sis.

- People say you are a bit much.

- I get it; they told you to keep quiet.

- I understand you have struggled with self-doubt and insecurities...

- But He needs your voice and your boldness.

- There is a bound generation that needs you to go before the King at this hour.

- You were never told to play it safe.

- You have always been a different breed.

- When others misunderstood your passion, God was building your voice.

- When others overlooked you, you were bathing in the oil.

- When others settled for a title, you were being prepared for a crown.

- Because: You stood out, and that is why you never quite fit in.

- Sugar, spice, and everything nice did not create you.

- Something did not create you to fit the mold.

- God called you and separated you.

-As a wailing woman of Zion, he needs you.

-Your requirements to the enemy's camp: You must drive a tent peg into the enemy camp. (Military strategies)

- You need to take that scarlet thread and wrap it around your home.

- Take the tambourine and lead the march to freedom; that is what He needs you to do.

- Taking on this tough challenge requires His help.

- Empty your alabaster jar for him.

- The world needs to hear His word, and He needs you to carry it.

- He urges you to speak out loud, like a trumpet, to encourage those who come after you.

Arise Esther.

Silence is no loger an option.

You are the voice of a generation.

Chapter 9 | Walking In Your Esther Moment

Imagine knowing that the fate of an entire nation rested on your shoulders, with everything hanging on your courageous "yes" to God.

Esther understood this weight like no one else. She was the ultimate underdog—a young Jewish woman in a foreign land, hidden behind layers of secrecy and uncertainty. Despite the odds, she found herself thrust into the heart of the king's court, enduring months of grueling beauty treatments and challenges. Yet, amid it all, he miraculously chose her, favoring her above all others to become queen.

This was not just a story of survival; it was a divine setup for a monumental purpose. Esther's journey reminds us that even when we feel like we are the least likely candidate, God can position us in places of influence to fulfill His plans.

But the favor in Esther's life was not just for her own benefit—it was for something far greater.

God handpicked her to be the deliverer of His people, the Jews, from a diabolical plot of genocide. This was a task that required more than just courage; it demanded the influence and favor that only a queen in close standing with a powerful king could wield.

As I reflected on Esther's story recently, Holy Spirit brought a prophetic revelation to my heart, reminding me of Esther 4:14:

Esther's story is a powerful reminder that God's favor in our lives often positions us to fulfill purposes that reach far beyond ourselves.

Esther 4:14 (NIV) states:

> *"For if you remain silent at this time, relief and deliverance for the Jews will arise from another place, but you and your father's family will perish. And who knows but that you have come to your royal position for such a time as this?"*

This verse, spoken by Mordecai to Esther, highlights the urgency of the moment and the pivotal role that Esther plays in God's plan.

We should remember that our positions and opportunities may benefit a greater purpose, not just ourselves.

It is her deciding moment: will she step into destiny? Will she face potential death to save her people?

As I pondered this moment from Esther's story, I wondered about its significance for us today.

Step Into Your Esther Moment!

Like Esther, God is preparing us for our own divine Kairos moments. Kairos time is when we suddenly enter God's miraculous timing to see a shift or break through occur.

Kairos is an ancient Greek word for a special, opportune moment. Unlike Chronos, which measures regular time (like seconds, minutes, and hours), Kairos represents a significant opportunity. It's a divinely appointed time when God will intersect with human actions.

In Christian thought, Kairos time is a period when God intervenes powerfully, bringing change, breakthroughs, or divine help. It is a special moment when something profound can happen, and it requires a response of faith and action.

5 ways to step into your Esther Moment

ACCEPT YOUR CALLING!

- Esther had every reason to disqualify herself from her royal position. Her Jewish heritage should have prevented them from bringing her into the palace. However, when God calls us, he qualifies us. He makes a way where there is no way. And He makes beautiful stories out of the chaos of it all!
- What is the destiny God is calling you to step into in this season? Is there a dream, a skill, a mission He has put on your heart - but you have been putting it off out of fear? If you are facing a massive obstacle or challenge... that may be the very thing God wants to use to set you up for a miracle.
- It is time to let go of fear and say "yes" as you step into your God-given destiny.

Bravely obey God!

- Esther had a tough choice to make. She could not just think about the ramifications on herself - she had to think of how her action - or inaction - would affect her entire people group! She obeyed God, and that took bravery.
- Like Esther, God will often ask us to do hard and holy things. This is part of our sanctification process. It is part of consecrating ourselves to him and his purposes. What if God is calling you to obey Him - because there is someone - or an entire group of people - that your obedience to God will affect? Your "yes" to God is not just about you - it is about those God wants to touch through your life. You have a glorious calling.

Speak up!

- Mordecai's challenge to Esther began with, "If you remain silent..." Esther had a choice: she could either use her voice or passively sit by and watch her people die.
- Have you ever let fear keep you from using your voice? Perhaps you sought to maintain peace. Maybe you were afraid of being misunderstood. Maybe something intimidated you into silence. I want to encourage you that God has given you a voice for a reason! In the times we are in, it will take more and more boldness to speak up - but that is exactly what God is calling us to.

Resolve To Take The Leap Of Faith

Regardless The Outcome!

- Esther knew what she had to do. Here is her response to her uncle in Esther 4:16:

"Go, gather all the Jews that are present in Shushan, and fast for me; and neither eat nor drink for three days, night or day. I also and my maids will fast as you do. Then I will go to the king, though it is against the law; and if I perish, I perish."

If I die, I die.

- This was it. Esther had resolved what she would do. She must approach the king with her unlawful request.
- It is here that we realize God may ask us to go against the culture of the day. Could it be that God is raising up deliverers who will seek His will that will not seem "lawful" in our times? But what if their bravery will save the lives of many and shift the course of nations? Will we choose to fear man - or God?
- Trust me, I know it is a tall order. Facing prison? Death?
- We may face other giants: being rejected by friends and family or slander and ridicule.
- If God calls you to boldness in your workplace, community, city, and nation, He will give you the strength and joy to obey. He is looking for willing and weak vessels that He can empower with boldness to affect the nations - so why not you?

- Jesus is worthy, and any cost he asks us to pay is worth it for the sake of His plan.

LET GOD DEAL WITH YOUR ENEMIES!

Here was the original plot the wicked Haman devised: "to destroy, eliminate and annihilate all the Jews, young and old, infants and women, in a single day."

Skipping ahead in the story, Haman hung on the very gallows he created for Mordecai. And Mordecai? He got the royal treatment that Haman was planning for himself!

When we choose to follow God's way and let Him give us vengeance and justice, the results will be supernaturally miraculous. He IS and always has been a righteous and just judge. His justice may seem late, but He has perfect timing. Obey God and trust Him with the outcome of the injustice you are facing! He specializes in writing exciting plot twists and good endings.

As we reflect on the miraculous justice of God, let us turn our attention to the limitless potential He has placed within each of us. Imagine living with no limitations—no fears, no obstacles, just pure potential. What would this mean for the call God has on your life? It would be a transformation beyond measure. The next chapter will give insight to live this life.

Chapter 10 | A Personal Call to Action

Imagine living with no limitations—no fears, no obstacles, just pure potential. What would this mean for the call God has on *your* life? It would be a transformation beyond measure. Here's how:

Understanding the Edict

Jeremiah 29:11: For I know the plans I have for you, declares the Lord, plans to prosper you and not to harm you, plans to give you hope and a future.

2 Corinthians 4:17-18: For our light and momentary troubles are achieving for us an eternal glory that far outweighs them all. We focus, then, not on the visible, but on the invisible, for the visible is temporary, while the invisible is eternal.

Paul encourages us to look beyond earthly limitations and focus on the eternal glory that God has prepared for us.

UNLEASHED PURPOSE

With no limitations, you could embrace the purpose God has designed for you. Every dream and vision placed in your heart would be within reach, and you could pursue it with unwavering confidence.

Boundless Faith

Your faith would soar to new heights, unencumbered by doubt or fear. You would trust God's promises wholeheartedly, knowing that nothing is impossible for Him.

"Not one promise from God is empty of power, for nothing is

impossible with God." Luke 1:37 TPT

Impactful Ministry

Your ministry would grow rapidly, touching lives in unexpected ways. Without limits, you could reach more people, inspire greater change, and build stronger communities of faith.

> *"Your lives light up the world. For how can you hide a city that stands on a hilltop? And who would light a lamp and then hide it in an obscure place? Instead, it's placed where everyone in the house can benefit from its light. So don't hide your light! Let it shine brightly before others, so that the commendable things you do will shine as light upon them, and then they will give their praise to your Father in heaven." Matthew 5:14-16 TPT.*

Creative Expression

Your creativity would flourish if freed from constraints. You could express your gifts and talents in unique and powerful ways, glorifying God through every endeavor.

> *"We have become his poetry, a re-created people that will fulfill*

the destiny He has given each of us, for we are joined to Jesus, the Anointed One. Even before we were born, God planned our destiny and the good works we would do to fulfill it!"
Ephesians 2:10 TPT

This passage beautifully highlights how we are God's creative masterpiece, designed to fulfill our unique destiny and purpose.

DEEPER RELATIONSHIPS

Without the barriers of insecurity or fear, your relationships would deepen. You could connect with others on a more profound level, offering love, support, and encouragement as you walk together in faith.

"Two are better than one, for they can help each other succeed. If one person falls, the other can reach out and help. But someone who falls alone is in real trouble. Likewise, two people lying close together can keep each other warm. But how can one be warm alone? Two people standing back-to-back can defeat an attacker. A three-stranded cord is even stronger, and not easily broken." Ecclesiastes 4:9 - 12 TPT.

LEGACY OF HOPE

Living without limits, your life would inspire hope and future generations. Your journey would show God's power and faithfulness, encouraging others to follow their divine callings.

Embracing a life without limitations means stepping into the divine call God has in your life. This will affect the world with His love, and fulfilling the unique mission He has entrusted to you.

"Now may God, the fountain of hope, fill you to overflowing with uncontainable joy and perfect peace as you trust in Him. And may the power of the Holy Spirit continually surround your life with His super-abundance until you radiate with hope!" Romans 15:13 TPT.

Do you feel ready to explore this limitless potential? How would you like to begin this journey? After Esther bravely approached the king and revealed Haman's wicked plot, the king issued a new edict. This second edict granted the Jews the right to defend themselves, a significant moment that turned their impending doom into a victory.

For us today, this represents the shift that can occur when we step into our calling and align ourselves with God's purposes. Just as the original edict of destruction was reversed by Esther's obedience, we too have the authority, through Christ, to overturn the plans of the enemy.

*What is the **edict** in your life?*

But it requires action. Esther didn't just pray and fast; she spoke up and took courageous steps, despite the risks. Similarly, God may call you to act, to speak up, or to step out of faith in an area where you see the enemy's plans at work. Your obedience could be the key to unlocking freedom, not just for yourself, but for those around you.

What area is God calling you to address, to overturn, or to declare His truth?

Just as Esther's courage shifted the course of history for her people, your boldness in following God can create ripples of change in your community, your family, and beyond.

Choosing a life goal is like creating a personal branding guide that will lead your decisions and actions. Let me challenge you today to invest in yourself. Time is the most precious commodity we have and filling that time with space for The Father, Son and Holy Spirit are the investments that will negotiate all closed doors or barren wombs. Also, take time to invest in what Yahweh has to say about you; write the vision plainly, and then tell someone about who you are and who God says you are without hesitation. These will be testimonies to your lineage until the Lord's return.

1. Reflect on Your Values

   - Identify what is most important to you. Consider your core values, such as integrity, compassion, faith, creativity, or community. These values will be the foundation of your life's edict.

2. Determine Your Purposes

- Think about your long-term goals and what you feel called to do. This could be your vocation, personal mission, or spiritual calling. Reflect on questions such as, "What do I want to achieve?" and "How do I want to contribute to the world?"

3. Set Clear Intentions

- Outline specific intentions that align with your values and purpose. These intentions will guide your daily actions and decisions. Make sure they are realistic and actionable.

4. Draft Your Edict

- Write a concise and clear statement that encapsulates your values, purpose, and intentions. Use positive language and focus on what you want to achieve. Here's a simple format:

"I am committed to [values] by [specific actions] in order to Fulfill My [purpose]."

- Example:

"I am committed to living a life of integrity and compassion by helping others and seeking personal growth in order to make a positive impact in my community."

5. Review and Revise

- Take time to review your edict and make any necessary adjustments. Ensure it resonates deeply with you and reflects your true aspirations. It should be both inspiring and attainable.

6. Live It Out

- Use your edict as a guiding principle for your daily life. Reflect on it regularly to stay aligned with your goals and values. Let it shape your decisions, actions, and interactions with others.

7. Adapt as Needed

- Life is dynamic, and your edict may strengthen. Be open to revisiting and revising it as you grow and as your circumstances change.

Creating a life edict helps you stay focused and intentional. It is a living declaration that can inspire and guide you to fulfill your purpose and make a meaningful impact.

PS I would absolutely love to hear your story! Connect with me on Facebook or any social media platform and share your journey with the world.

THE JOY OF THE LORD IS YOUR STRENGTH!

The feast of Purim falls in the Jewish month of Adar, which speaks of strength. This month also has a traditional saying that goes with it: when the month of Adar arrives, we increase in joy. Therefore, the month of Adar and the feast of Purim suggest that "the joy of the Lord is our strength". What a perfect reminder of that season!

> *As for the American month of Adar, Adar typically falls between February and March. In 2024, the Feast of Purim was on the evening of March 23rd and ended on March 24th. Adar is a month of joy and celebration, a reminder of the strength and victory we have in the Lord, just as the Jews celebrated their deliverance from Haman's plot.*

Reflecting on this, we can see that our lives, like Esther's, are not just for our own benefit. We are called to be vessels of God's purposes, affecting others through our faith, courage, and obedience. Whether facing personal challenges or standing up for others, our decisions have far-reaching consequences, just as Esther did.

It's called the Feast of Lots because Haman used a lottery to pick the date for the annihilation of the Jews. This is a rather interesting fact. His plan failed, and with Purim, we have been celebrating ever since!

So, what is the prophetic significance of us and how can we practically apply it to our lives today?

Like Esther, God is calling you to greatness for the times we are in. His joy will be your strength as you step into the divine moment, He is preparing you for.

While it may seem dark outside, God is making his people ready to arise and shine for His glory. I expect to see God's power bring awakening and revival. I'm preparing myself to be used by Him; aren't you?

> *"Lord, whatever you are doing in this season. Don't do it without me!"*
>
> *Give God a renewed "yes" today and watch what He does in and through you!*
>
> *But we are just getting started.*

It's incredible how God took a simple girl from North Georgia and gave her the power to write such moving words. I pray these words are a profound blessing to so many. This contrast highlights the girl's simple life, marked by quiet routines and unassuming surroundings, against the power and depth of her words.

Unbelievable! This day, once a distant dream, is finally here, a tangible reality filled with the nervous energy of anticipation.

CHAPTER 10 | A PERSONAL CALL TO ACTION

Incredible experiences, all blessings from God, have filled my life. These include amazing places and inspiring people.

In my upcoming books, I will delve into the rich tapestry of my history, revealing the pivotal moments that have shaped our journey to this point. Vivid details, from the scent of wood-smoke to the sting of tears, and emotional depth will fill the stories, resonating long after you finish reading. Your ministry mirrors your past, creating a connection you deeply comprehend and cherish.

This exploration will examine abuse, and divorce, along with the profound influence of love. My experiences with multiple divorces and the ambiguities of marriage will be detailed.

In addition, we could delve into the harrowing experience of facing a 12-gauge shotgun head-on or the devastating impact of childhood rape. Should we delve into the specific location and dissect how these events transpired so subtly, hidden from the elders' watchful eyes?

THE END, For Now...

Acknowledgements

Above all, my heart overflows with gratitude to God (Yahweh) for His saving grace. Instrumental to my success has been your guidance and words, even during moments of quiet reflection.

Our vocabulary cannot touch the splendor you deserve, as words seem inadequate. Words seem inadequate to capture the true essence of your magnificence and grandeur. We fall short in describing the splendor of which you are worthy. Language itself seems insufficient to convey the depth of your beauty and brilliance.

Your profound awesomeness inspires awe in others. It is impossible for anyone to comprehend the extent of your incredible qualities. It's impossible for anyone to understand the abundant grace You have repeatedly shown me. Your abundant grace is truly beyond my comprehension, leaving me awestruck each time. He has worked through so many people to bring me to this point in my life, and I am deeply grateful.

To my husband, David Mierez, thank you for always helping me when the days were tough. Unwavering support, love, and encouragement:

these have been my constant source of strength. You make me feel beautiful on my worst days, and I deeply appreciate your concern for every step I take in the ministry that God has placed in my hands.

To my mom and dad, your belief in me has been a guiding light. Mom, you always told me I could, cheered me on when I was in the corner alone, and never let me stay down. Your actions made me feel like I towered above everyone else in the room. Because of your unwavering support and constant encouragement, Dad, you have been a guiding light in my life, always lifting me up when I needed it most. Your love, support, and guidance were foundational to me. I could not have come this far without the love, support, and guidance from both of you, which have been my foundation and strength.

Savannah, my daughter, possesses a God-given beauty that she embraces fully, her confidence palpable and inspiring. Because of your courageous and public declaration of self-ownership, my dear, I offer my deepest admiration.

Savannah, you are a beacon of strength and grace. Despite facing challenges, your journey of self-discovery is a testament to your unwavering faith and resilience. Inner beauty, not mere physical attractiveness, defines you, showcasing your soul. With your radiating confidence, you illuminate each room you enter and inspire everyone around you to embrace their own unique beauty.

Boldly declaring your own identity, you defy a world that often tries to define you. Importantly, your journey powerfully reminds us that true beauty comes from within, and that, importantly, we are all beautifully and wonderfully made. Your narrative, a testament to transformation, unfolds even as the complete story remains untold, much like a butterfly emerging from its cocoon, ready to soar.

My dear child, walk in your God-given purpose, knowing that many love, cherish, and admire you. Your courage and authenticity are a gift to the world, and I am incredibly proud to call you, my daughter. Keep shining, keep inspiring, and never forget that you are a masterpiece in the making.

Elijah, my grandson who continues to amaze and motivate me to greater heights and deeper completion. I cannot wait to see what Yahweh ignites through you!

To Kasie Reynolds Barrett, thank you for not allowing me to fail. Your relentless push towards the truth and the correct direction has been invaluable. Your faith in me and your guidance were pivotal in this journey.

Pastors Jimmy and Sharon Harper, your encouragement was a lifeline when I felt devoid of inspiration and unable to offer anything more; thank you. The words hung in the air that Sunday morning, a challenge and a comfort: "Keep writing, anyway."

To all the unnamed souls who have touched my life and played a role in my journey, I thank you. Your contributions, no matter how small, have not gone unnoticed.

With heartfelt gratitude,

Tonia Dockery-Mierez

www.ingramcontent.com/pod-product-compliance
Lightning Source LLC
Chambersburg PA
CBHW071124090426
42736CB00012B/1999